Counting Starfish

Counting Book For Children
Coloring Book Included

Brenda J. Sullivan
Kathryn A. Sullivan

Counting Starfish

Second Edition Print

ISBN: 978-1-7329990-1-5

Published by Tree Roots Press

Photography
Brenda J. Sullivan
Artwork
Brenda J. Sullivan
Kathryn A. Sullivan
Google Images - Crown of Thorns Sea Star

Requests to publish work from this book should be sent to:
Treerootspress@gmail.com
brenda@brendajsullivanbooks.com

treerootspress.com

Dedicated to sea stars that live in the wild

Picture of a wild sea star off the coast of Alaska

Katie with Mommy being silly while we paint   Katie with Daddy on one of our beach walks

Katie finishing up one of her whale pictures. Yes, we paint outside the lines!

Meet the Artist!

Katie

Katie is a wheelchair-bound young lady with severe cerebral palsy and epilepsy among many other medical problems. She is also nonverbal with very limited vision. Despite these challenges, she has a fighting spirit and has learned how to use basic communication skills and assistive technology to produce various arts and craft products.

This is one of Katie's "Able Gifts" – a product she's helped create with her Mother, Brenda J. Sullivan, when she is in good health and "able" to do so. Proceeds from these books are used to support the costs of Katie's craft-works and enable her to more fully engage her world.

Katie is excited when a whale swims by the window at the sea aquarium

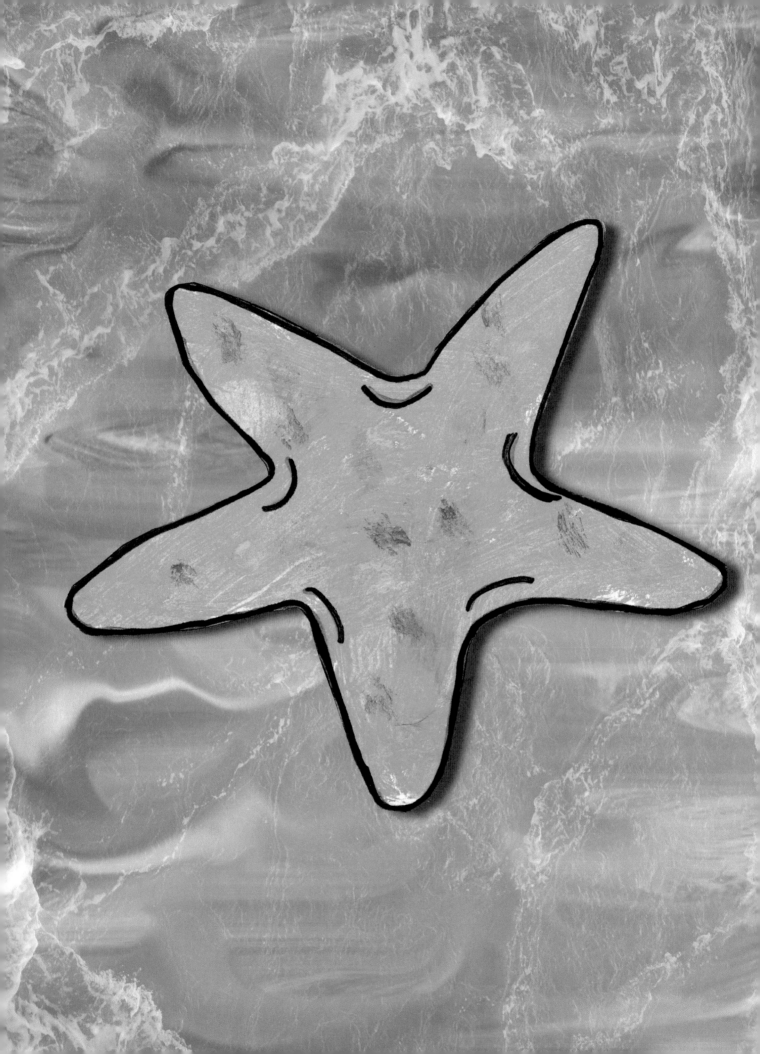

1

One Starfish

2

Two Starfish

3

Three Starfish

4

Four Starfish

5
Five Starfish

Six Starfish

7

Seven Starfish

Eight Starfish

9

Nine Starfish

10

Ten Starfish

Purple and orange sea stars found in the wild off the coast of Alaska. They are creeping out of the water and up the rocks using the suckers under their arms.

Look at the underside of this big sea star! Do you see the little clam shell attached to it? Its suckers pulled the clam out of its shell and ate it for lunch.

This sea star was found in the wild off the coast of Alaska.

This sea star, called Crown of Thorns, lives in the Indian and Pacific Oceans but is mostly found in Australia. They can grow as big as 10 - 14 inches (25 to 35 cm) and can have up to 23 arms!

Fun Facts About Starfish

- Starfish are actually Sea Stars. They come from the invertebrate family (meaning they have no backbones) and are not really fish.

- Sea Stars come in many different colors and can grow as many as 50 arms in their lifetime. If one of their arms gets broken off, they grow another one to replace it.

- Sea Stars don't swim or walk but creep along the ocean floor and rocks with little suckers, which are suction cups under their arms.

- Sea Stars can live in all types of habitats including very cold waters and very warm waters around the world. They can also live in kelp beds and in coral reefs.

1

One Starfish

2

Two Starfish

Three Starfish

4

Four Starfish

5

Five Starfish

6

Six Starfish

7

Seven Starfish

8

Eight Starfish

Nine Starfish

10

Ten Starfish

About Our Family

Brenda Sullivan lives in South Glastonbury, CT with her husband Paul and their daughter Katie.

They are avid nature lovers and gardeners who took their love of gardening to a new level by converting their 1.3 acres into a small farm called Thompson Street Farm LLC.

Brenda is an herbalist and market gardener who specializes in growing lavender, medicinal herbs and flowers. She also makes handcrafted goat's milk herbal soaps and herbal bath products using the herbs, flowers, fruits and vegetables grown on their farm or purchased from other local farmers.

More information on her bath and body products can be found at www.farmtobath.com

Katie, the love of their life and the center of their universe, has a number of serious medical conditions including severe cerebral palsy, epilepsy and very limited vision. She is nonverbal and wheelchair bound but these challenges have not prevented Katie from experiencing life.

Katie experiences the world on her terms with the help of assistive technology, other sensory, adaptations and years of homeschooling experience. Katie understands basic concepts and has developed many interests including an appreciation for music, painting with her Mother, and listening to stories.

She loves being outdoors and we've discovered that enabling her to experience the natural world has been Katie's best educator. This has been our inspiration for creating nature themed children's books.

Connect with Brenda online:
www.brendajsullivanbooks.com
www.thompsonstreetfarm.com
www.farmtobath.com
www.livingandlovinherbs.com
Facebook.com/brendajsullivanbooks
Facebook.com/livingandlovinherbspodcast

Other Books By Brenda J. Sullivan

Children's Books

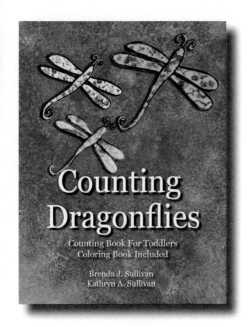

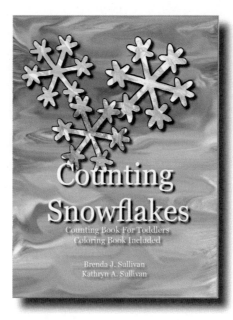

Available in all stores and libraries - just ask!

Journals

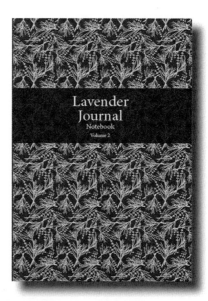

This journal has 22 pages of beautiful color pictures of lavender and wild life visiting our garden. An index is also included to reference favorite notes.

This journal has beautiful black and white lavender illustrations on all the pages. An index is also included to reference favorite notes.

Made in the USA
Coppell, TX
17 July 2022